STIFTUNG
PREUSSISCHE SCHLÖSSER UND GÄRTEN
BERLIN-BRANDENBURG

Rudolf G. Scharmann

Charlottenburg Palace

Royal Prussia in Berlin

Prestel

Munich · Berlin · London · New York

CONTENTS

Charlottenburg Palace: Prussian Splendour in Berlin

History and significance

In spite of devastating damage during the Second World War and a lengthy period of reconstruction, Charlottenburg is today the largest former residence of the Hohenzollern dynasty in the German capital.

Now a museum of international standing, it is a popular destination for excursions as well as a venue much in demand for cultural events and social functions alike.

A magnificent ensemble of buildings, interiors, artistic masterpieces and gardens provides a variety of insights into the history of the court of Brandenburg-Prussia from the Baroque period until the early 20th century. The turbulent architectural and social history of the extensive palace complex has been marked by numerous alterations during the 200 years of its existence, both as a royal residence and subsequent state administration, as well as by the ravages of war and lengthy reconstruction phases. On a cultural "journey through time", the visitor can directly experience 300 years of art and history in an authentic setting.

Standing in the Berlin district of Charlottenburg-Wilmersdorf, the splendid palace and garden complex not only displays the culture of the Brandenburg-Prussian monarchy, but also symbolizes the turbulence of German history from the 17th century to the present day. The complex is dominated by the Old Palace with its monumental domed tower visible far and wide. The Great Courtyard is flanked by two further wings. The Chapel to the left is adjoined by the Great Orangery, while to the right, parts of the New Wing can be seen. Behind the central section lies the Baroque formal garden with the Carp Pond beyond.

Charlottenburg Palace: The Beginnings

From an electoral hunting lodge to a royal summer palace—Sophie Charlotte's "Court of the Muses"

The original building, a small palace named Lietzenburg or Lützenburg, was erected between 1695 and 1699 not far from the village of Lietzow, which was one Brandenburg mile (about 7.5 kilometres) from the centre of Berlin. It was commissioned by Electress Sophie Charlotte, the second wife of Elector Frederick III of Brandenburg, who in 1701 declared himself "King Frederick I in Prussia". In its modest dimensions, based on Dutch exemplars, this little summer residence, built to the plans of Johann Arnold Nering, accorded with her wishes for a rural retreat away from the official court life of the City Palace in Berlin. However, once she had been elevated to the status of first "Queen in Prussia", she decided that the little Lietzenburg no longer adequately reflected her new position. Extensive enlargements based on the designs of the Swedish architect Johann Friedrich Eosander culminated in a splendid Baroque three-wing complex in line with the latest French taste. From 1701/02, the main axis

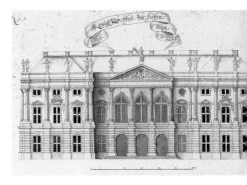

A drawing by C. Reichmann (fl. early 18th c.) of the view from the Lietzenburg courtyard in 1704 shows the original building by Johann Arnold Nering (1659–95) still without the tall domed tower begun in 1710/12. On 11 July 1699, Frederick III's birthday, the Palace was opened with splendid festivities ending in a fireworks display. The electoral couple and their guests had great fun, "leaping, so to speak, over tables and benches".

"She has big, gentle eyes, wonderfully thick black hair, eyebrows looking as if they had been drawn, a well-proportioned nose, incarnadine lips, very good teeth, and a lively complexion." The portrait of Sophia Charlotte painted in 1702/05 by Friedrich Wilhelm Weidemann (1668–1750) confirms contemporary opinion of her imposing appearance. As the daughter of Duke Ernest Augustus of Brunswick-Lüneburg and his consort Sophia of the Palatinate, when this picture was painted she had been married for dynastic reasons in 1684 to the future Elector Frederick III of Brandenburg at Herrenhausen Palace in Hanover. Sophia Charlotte was a piece of great good fortune for the up-and-coming princely capital of Berlin. She brought cosmopolitan flair, taste and charm to the electoral court. Having sought at first to promote her family's political aims, after being crowned first Prussian Queen in 1701 she retreated to the domain of intellectual leadership at Lietzenburg.

Johann Böcklin (fl. early 18th c.) created this view of Charlottenburg from the courtyard side on the basis of drawings by Johann Friedrich Eosander (1669–1728). The Great Courtyard with its imposing approach for prominent guests takes account of the greater demands of court ceremonial following the elevation of the elector to royal status.

was extended both to the east and to the west, and provided on the garden side with a prestigious show-façade on the model of Louis XIV's palace at Versailles.

The Great Courtyard on the city side is enclosed by two further wings at right angles to the main building, guard-houses, and wrought-iron railings crowned by the stars of the Prussian Order of the Black Eagle. It was in this courtyard that the equestrian statue of the "Great Elector" Frederick William of Brandenburg (Frederick III's father) was re-erected in 1951 after spending the war years in storage. The central section of the original palace is dominated by the domed tower, approximately 50 metres tall, with its lantern topped by a

The first official portrait of Frederick III as the new Elector of Brandenburg, painted c.1688 by Gedeon Romandon (d. 1697), already gives some inkling of the ruler's desire for a crown.

The statue of the Great Elector, commissioned by Frederick III to honour the achievements of his father, was modelled by Andreas Schlüter (1659–1714) between 1697 and 1700, and cast by Johann Jacobi (1661–1726). It originally stood on the Long Bridge in the grounds of the Berlin City Palace and is one of Europe's most important equestrian statues. The four slaves chained to the base of the plinth, added only in 1708/09, symbolize the four humours and the enemies subjugated by the Great Elector.

The regular alternation of slender mirrors with green damask in the Glass Bedchamber of Sophia Charlotte's First Apartment (room 118) brings an illusion of the garden into the room. Today, magnificently carved and gilt display furniture, along with a silver mirror from Augsburg, still recall the original elaborate splendour.

weather-vane in the form of a gilded figure of Fortuna, the goddess of good luck. Two orangeries were planned as winter quarters for citrus plants, but only the Great Orangery on the western side was actually built, being completed in 1712. In place of the planned eastern

orangery, Frederick the Great had the New Wing erected as a summer palace, before deciding that he preferred Sanssouci in Potsdam. Since 1977 a bronze statue of the king, after a 1792 marble original by Johann Gottfried Schadow, has stood in front of this New Wing.

Sophia Charlotte's Lietzenburg was not an official summer residence, but her private retreat. The rooms are decorated with damask and brocade hangings in different colours, while Far

In the Writing Cabinet of Sophia Charlotte's Second Apartment (room 112) her white lacquer writing-desk with its chinoiserie painting is still extant. Made probably in Holland c.1700, it is an expression of a sensuous and exotically fantastic dream world, which, as a fashion for all things Chinese, was to be a model for Europe's courtly society for more than 100 years.

Right: The copy of the statue of Frederick the Great after Johann Gottfried Schadow (1764–1850) in front of the New Wing shows the king as general, legislator and peacemaker.

Eastern porcelain and exotically painted lacquer furniture are in tune with the then prevailing fashion for chinoiserie. The ceilings of Nering's First Apartment for Sophia Charlotte are characterized by gilt plasterwork, while Eosander's Second Apartment reflects the new, French-influenced taste for ceiling-paintings. It was the express wish of the electress that high glazed doors provide direct access from the built architecture to the elaborately designed "nature" of the gardens.

The daily routine of Sophia Charlotte's predominantly youthful courtiers and guests was characterized by relaxed parties, balls, garden festivals and

The elaborate but delicate ceiling painting of the Golden Cabinet in Sophia Charlotte's Second Apartment (room 109) depicts figurative representations in the then (c. 1700) highly modern French style, with its vegetal running motifs. The god Apollo, hovering on the clouds in the centre, is surrounded by the allegories of music, poetry, architecture and painting—a mythological image of the earthly court of the muses maintained by the chatelaine of Charlottenburg.

In 1846 Adolph Menzel (1815–1905) illustrated the famous "philosophical strolls" which Sophia Charlotte took in the company of Leibniz in the Lietzenburg palace gardens. The conversations are said to have inspired one of the scholar's major works, the "Théodicée", to answer the question of how a loving and omnipotent God can permit evil in the world. Time and again the knowledge-hungry queen had posed this question.

masquerades. At the same time, the electress and later queen would engage in discussion of the philosophical topics of the day with renowned scholars and theologians. She succeeded in enticing her childhood tutor, the polymath Gottfried Wilhelm Leibniz, to Berlin, and in 1700 the two of them persuaded the elector to found the Academy of Sciences. Her particular passion and talent, however, lay in the field of music, above all Italian opera, performances of which she sometimes accompanied herself on the harpsichord. Well-known composers such as Attilio Ariosti and Giovanni Bononcini would spend time "on loan" to her court.

During a tour of France lasting several months in the company of her mother, the future Electress Sophia of Hanover, which also included sojourns in Paris and Versailles, the 11-year-old Sophia Charlotte was the guest of her cousin and godmother Elisabeth Charlotte of Orleans. A German princess, originally Liselotte of the Palatinate, this sister-in-law of Louis XIV was regarded as a connoisseur of modern fashions. In her extensive, in some cases sharp-tongued and less-than-genteel letters to her relations at home, she presented a lively picture of life at the French court. Louis Elle (1648–1717) portrayed her in 1673 in hunting gear, the costume of her favourite pastime.

Extensions to the building after elevation to royal status led Sophia Charlotte to abandon her First Apartment on the garden side and to establish herself in 1702 in a Second Apartment on the side facing the courtyard. In the Golden Cabinet (room 109) there is a youthful portrait of her above the fireplace. It may well have been painted during her tour of France in 1679. Delicate lacquer furniture in the Chinese style underline the private character of this intimate room.

Sophia Charlotte's white harpsichord is on display at Charlottenburg (room 103) as the most valuable token of her enthusiasm for music. It was built by the Berlin court instrument-maker Michael Mietke (d. 1719), the coloured chinoiserie painting being attributed to Gerard Dagly (fl. 1697–1714). In 1702, the queen wrote to the director of music in Hanover, Agostino Steffani, about music thus: "It is a loyal friend that never leaves one and never deceives one, it never betrays one and has never been cruel. On the contrary, all the charm and delight of heaven is there. Friends by contrast are lukewarm or unreliable, and lovers ungrateful."

Top left: Among the extant contents of the Toilet Chamber in Sophia Charlotte's Second Apartment (room 110) are portraits of foreign or unusual personalities—an indication of the queen's tolerance and cosmopolitanism. Of particular importance are the portraits in the bottom row of Matveyeva, the wife of the Russian ambassador, the Greek Orthodox bishop Vidola, and the maid of honour von Pöllnitz, who was a close friend and confidante of Sophia Charlotte.

The light background of the in part original ceiling of the Toilet Chamber in Sophia Charlotte's Second Apartment (room 110) is covered by grotesques painted in tempera. These novel ceiling compositions, based on the style of the French painters Jean Berain I (1640–1711) and Claude Audran III (1658–1734), must surely have been executed at the behest of the "francophile" queen.

The portrait of the crown prince Frederick William, the future "soldier king", painted in 1702 by Anthoni Schoonjans (1655–1726), depicting the heir to the throne as David with a sling, is part of the original decoration of the bedroom of his mother Sophia Charlotte in her Second Apartment. Both a portrait and an historical picture, the depiction links the Old Testament shepherd boy with the archetypal Baroque display portrait, with the purpose of conveying a political message: just as David was God's chosen successor to the throne, so Frederick William was God's chosen crown prince for Prussia.

Bottom left: In 1697 Sophia Charlotte succeeded in enticing the Italian composer and instrumentalist Attilio Ariosti, a Servite monk, to her court. In 1702 he was portrayed by Anthoni Schoonjans (1655–1726) seated at a lacquer harpsichord decorated in the Chinese style.

Charlottenburg Palace up to 1713

Baroque magnificence – the Old Palace as the country residence of King Frederick I

Following the early death of the "philosopher queen" Sophia Charlotte – she died in 1705 aged just 37 – the lights went out on the cultural life of the Lietzenburg. In honour of his late consort, King Frederick I – as he now was – renamed the palace Charlottenburg. The little settlement that had grown up in front of it was given municipal privileges and also named Charlottenburg. From then on until his death in 1713, it became his favourite country residence, also providing a venue for official state functions such as chivalric ceremonies and audiences with ambassadors, which hitherto had been reserved for the City Palace in Berlin. In 1702, even before the queen's death, considerable alterations to the palace interior had been initiated. On the French model, a strict hierarchy of rooms provided the framework for the requirements of ceremony. The state rooms, which included, in addition to the ballrooms, galleries and audience chambers, also the king's study, bedroom and bathroom, were in some cases provided with anterooms, designed to emphasize the distance between the monarch and those requesting an audience. The Palace Chapel symbolized the link between throne and altar, characteristic of the Prussian ruling house. In order to enhance the unfolding magnificence and the display of power, the rooms were arranged in an enfilade, in other words, all the doors were along a single axis, so that all 13 rooms on the garden side can be traversed in a straight line. The culmination of the 140-metre enfilade is the famous Porcelain Cabinet designed by Eosander, created with the intention of impressing visitors with an overwhelming abundance of Far Eastern porcelain displayed in geometric architectural fashion.

Right: In c.1712 the court painter Antoine Pesne (1683–1757) was summoned from France to paint a splendid Baroque state portrait of King Frederick I with his royal insignia on the silver throne. While still Elector of Brandenburg, he realized that only as king would he be taken seriously by other European monarchs. On 18 January 1701 he crowned himself "King in Prussia", thus achieving his goal. He had more than 20 summer residences erected around Berlin, and commissioned the magnificent extensions to Charlottenburg.

The Prussian crown jewels, made in Berlin c.1700 for the coronation in Königsberg in 1701, are today kept in the Crown Cabinet (room 236) at Charlottenburg. They include the solid gold frames of the crowns of Frederick and Sophia Charlotte, which were once ornamented with precious stones, pearls and diamonds. As the jewels were repeatedly removed in order to present them to members of the royal house for "other purposes", over the years they were lost. The body of the diamond-studded eagle at the top of the sceptre is formed by a magnificent ruby, probably a gift from Tsar Peter I of Russia. The blue enamel orb, crowned by a cross, is enclosed in bands of gold studded with jewels.

From 2 to 16 July 1709, Frederick I received a state visit from Elector Augustus I (known as "the Strong") of Saxony—for a time he was also King Augustus II of Poland—and King Frederick IV of Denmark. The aim of the meeting was a defensive alliance directed at the king of Sweden. During this illustrious visit, courtly entertainments were held in Berlin, Potsdam, Caputh, Oranienburg and Charlottenburg. In memory of the important occasion, Frederick I commissioned Samuel Theodor Gericke (1665–1730) to paint a joint portrait, which was hung in Charlottenburg Palace. It documents not only the political alliance of the three rulers, but also the reception of Prussia into the circle of the venerable monarchies of Europe.

By erecting magnificent buildings, Frederick I saw his rule immortalized. As early as 1698, with his impending coronation in view, he commissioned Andreas Schlüter (c.1659–1714) and Johann Friedrich Eosander (1669–1728) to draw up plans for the rebuilding of the Berlin City Palace, the old chief seat of the Hohenzollern dynasty, as the most important Baroque residence north of the Alps. The dome, constructed by Friedrich August Stüler (1800–1865) between 1844 and 1852, was visible from afar and gave the Palace its characteristic appearance until the wartime bombing and the subsequent demolition of the building in 1950. After the destruction of the City Palace it fell to Charlottenburg to "deputize" for it. A model kept at Charlottenburg (room 123) still recalls the most important palace of the House of Hohenzollern.

Following the serious damage sustained in the war, the ceiling decoration of Frederick I's Audience Chamber (room 101) was restored between 1975 and 1977. The groups of white figures symbolize learning and the arts. Brussels tapestries woven c. 1730 depict scenes from Plutarch's lives of classical heroes. Lacquer furniture and Far Eastern porcelain underline the fascination of Baroque Europe with chinoiserie.

The oak carvings in the Old Gallery (room 120) were probably executed by an Englishman, Charles King (d. 1756). In rough chronological order, oval portraits of members of the House of Hohenzollern, from the first Elector of Brandenburg to Frederick the Great and his consort Elisabeth Christine, adorn a hall which is also known as the Ancestral Gallery. The chimney-breast is dominated by the full-length portrait of Frederick I, surrounded by his three consorts Elisabeth Henrietta of Hesse-Kassel, Sophia Charlotte of Hanover and Sophia Louisa of Mecklenburg-Schwerin-Grabow.

The magnificent gallery-like Red Chamber (room 100) was probably used as a conference room by Frederick I and his ministers. The walls are hung with red damask wallpaper and gold braid. Above the doors there are portraits of the royal couple, while in the panels at the base of the walls the Prussian Eagle and the Horse of Hanover frame the monogram of Sophia Charlotte in reference to the marital alliance of the two dynasties.

The Baroque state rooms also include the King's Bedroom (room 96). A remarkable feature here is the weather vane on the chimney-breast. In the adjoining Bathroom (room 97) oak-panelled walls surround the sunken white-marble basin, adorned with bronze taps in the form of dolphins. Between the two rooms there was a narrow passage used by the servants.

Right: 5 December 1706 saw the solemn consecration of the Charlottenburg Palace Chapel (room 94). Before her death Sophia Charlotte had approved the plans of Johann Friedrich Eosander (1669–1728). As the architect reported, she wanted "the place she dedicated to her God to be the most richly decorated of any in her palace". Opposite the royal gallery is the carved oaken pulpit, and beneath it the richly gilded communion table by Charles King (d. 1756). Above the royal gallery, which is separated from the Chapel by sliding windows, two hovering geniuses hold aloft a huge crown and Prussian Eagle to proclaim the glorious kingdom of Frederick I. This balanced presentation of temporal and spiritual power, of throne and altar, was in accord with the Reformed Calvinist faith of the Hohenzollern and their view of their divine right to rule. The ceiling painting executed in 1708 by Anthonie Coxcie (post 1650–c.1720), was totally reconstructed after its destruction in 1943 during the Second World War, as was the Chapel itself. The restored organ, dating from 1706, was built by Arp Schnitger (1648–1719).

The famous Charlottenburg Porcelain Cabinet (room 95)—the concept being the glorification of the rule of Frederick I and his newly created kingdom—is one of the oldest and at the same time largest of its kind in Germany. As an outstanding witness to the 18th-century fashion for chinoiserie, it was intended not only to impress the visitor with its extravagant abundance of porcelain, but also with the extent of

the kingdom's international relations as symbolized by the acquisitions. Reflections framed in gold multiply to great effect the unique collection of Chinese and Japanese treasures. Following enormous losses in the war, the current stock of porcelain comprises some 2,700 items, predominantly from the K'ang-hsi-period (1622–1722). The chief motif of the ceiling painting "Dawn Drives out the Darkness", executed in 1706 by Anthonie Coxcie (post 1650–c.1720) and seriously damaged in 1943, is the goddess Aurora surrounded by personifications of the continents, signs of the zodiac and allegories of the seasons.

The painting, executed by Dismar Degen (known to be alive c. 1730–1751) in c. 1739/40 shows the front of Monbijou Palace facing the River Spree. On the right in the background can be seen the tower of the still extant Sophia Church in the Mitte district of Berlin. In 1710 Sophia Dorothea was presented with the little jewel Monbijou by her father-in-law Frederick I. After 1877, the palace housed the Hohenzollern Museum. Following serious damage by air raids in 1943, the remains of the building were demolished between 1957 and 1960.

Some of the paintings, among them portraits of the queen's ladies-in-waiting, in Charlottenburg (room 228) recall Monbijou Palace, Sophia Dorothea and the royal family, as do certain items of furniture, for example the so-called "cradle of Frederick the Great".

The double portrait of the two-year-old crown prince Frederick (later Frederick the Great) and his sister Wilhelmine (1709–1758) was commissioned by Sophia Dorothea from Antoine Pesne (1683–1757). It shows her two eldest children, who throughout their lives were bound by ties of love, friendship and mutual reverence. While Frederick with his drum and the Prussian Order of the Eagle is intended to embody the "military element" of his future role as general and ruler, the gravely pacing five-year-old girl is carrying flowers, the attributes of femininity.

In this portrait painted c. 1733 in the studio of Antoine Pesne (1683–1757), Frederick William I is depicted as he liked to see himself, as a military commander with his staff of office.

Queen Sophia Dorothea, like her aunt Sophia Charlotte, was a scion of the proudly aristocratic House of Guelph. After a luxurious upbringing in Hanover, she found it hard to adjust to the parsimonious atmosphere at the Prussian court after her husband ascended the throne. She is shown here as the young crown princess in a portrait executed c. 1710 by Friedrich Wilhelm Weidemann (1668–1750).

On his death in 1713, Frederick I was succeeded by his son Frederick William I. At Charlottenburg, all new building activities were stopped, although maintenance work was continued as necessary. The parsimonious "soldier king" used the palace solely for receiving high-ranking state visitors and for magnificent family celebrations.

While the new king, whose tastes lay in the military and hunting spheres, invited his friends to come and smoke with him at his palace in Königs Wusterhausen, his consort Sophia Dorothea preferred the little summer residence of Monbijou, on the banks of the River Spree in Berlin. In this private retreat, with its fine collection of works of art, she created a "counter-culture" in which her ten children also spent periods of their childhood. In particular the crown prince (later King Frederick II) and his favourite sister Wilhelmine, the future margravine of Bayreuth, enjoyed the cultivated atmosphere of Monbijou. The unbridgeable difference in character between Frederick William I and his eldest son led to major tensions. In 1736, the latter was given permission to maintain his own court at Rheinsberg Palace. This place of literary, philosophical and musical study in the company of selected friends provided the pattern for Frederick's first seat of government when he ascended the throne in 1740: Charlottenburg.

Charlottenburg Palace in the 18th Century

Prussian Rococo – the New Wing as the residence of Frederick the Great

Immediately after succeeding his father in 1740, Frederick II, who was already being called "the Great" in his lifetime, commissioned the architect Georg Wenzeslaus von Knobelsdorff to build a New Wing to the east of the Old Palace at Charlottenburg. The king followed the building work with what patience he could muster. While campaigning in Silesia, he wrote to a friend: "I have had a letter from Knobelsdorff, with whom I am satisfied, but everything is too dry, it does not contain any details. I would like the description of every part of every column at Charlottenburg to take up four quarto pages, I would enjoy that."

By 1745, a long, two-storey building with a projecting central section was complete. There were 17 windows on each storey on either side of the central section, which itself was additionally emphasized by pairs of columns supporting a balcony, and vases at the base of the roof. In contrast to the discreetly reticent exterior, the interior of the New Wing was richly decorated: a high point of the Friderician Rococo characteristic of the period. Following an official invitation by the king, sculptors and decorators came to Prussia from all over Germany and beyond, among them Johann August Nahl the Elder, and the Hoppenhaupt brothers, the artistically most important decorators to work at Charlottenburg.

By 1742, Frederick II, with great personal commitment and interest, had had the First Apartment furnished, and by 1747 the Second Apartment.

An important design element in Frederick the Great's New Wing is the entrance portal with its ornamental columns and vases. These underline the autonomous character of this part of the complex as a residence in itself. The architectural creed of Georg Wenzeslaus von Knobelsdorff (1699–1753), whose varied use of the column motif is already in evidence at Rheinsberg, is developed further here.

In c.1740 Antoine Pesne (1683–1757) painted the young King Frederick II in a crimson coat with ermine trimmings, the sash of the Order of the Black Eagle, and a braided tricorn hat. The king, now about 28, comes across as mature and determined, deigning to give the beholder a condescending glance just for a moment.

In all the palaces occupied by Frederick II, the library was given particular importance, as here in the King's First Apartment, where, overlooking the garden, it is at the same time one of the most private and most sumptuous rooms (room 354). While the ceiling painting by Antoine Pesne (1683–1757) was destroyed in the war, the delicate green decor with silver-plated ornaments has been restored. In place of Frederick's collection of classical busts, the consoles above the simple cedarwood bookcases now hold plaster casts. The books are from the collection of the Potsdam City Palace. The table, part of the room's original furniture, conveys an idea of the elegance of this royal retreat.

The White Hall (room 362) was originally clad in pink stucco to create a marble effect, but this has since turned white. The design of the walls is purely architectural, which gives this room, used as a dining hall by Frederick the Great, a cool and austere appearance. Only the design of the doors leading to the adjoining banqueting hall conveys a more cheerful mood. Elegant and golden, the 'grotesque' variations on the Four Seasons invite guests to enter a different world, the weightlessness of the Golden Gallery.

Left: The gold ornamentation on the of light panelling in the Study (room 366) of the Second Apartment was doubtless executed to designs by the Hoppenhaupt brothers: Johann Michael (1709–post 1750) and Johann Christian (1719–between 1778 and 1786). In place of the original five 18th-century paintings set into the walls, there are now four large-format landscapes with genre scenes in the most elegant Rococo manner.

The former lay to the west, and the latter to the east, of the main staircase in the upper storey of the New Wing, and were connected by the White Hall and the Golden Gallery, an excitingly contrasting pair of state rooms. One of Frederick's favourite colours was gris-de-lin, a sort of mauve. The gris-de-lin damask hangings in the Gris-de-lin Room and the gilt frames of the carved and richly decorated corner cartouches have been restored. Today, the room is home to important paintings by French Rococo artists. Particularly worthy of mention is Watteau's masterpiece "Embarkment for Cythera" which was painted in 1718/19.

Even as crown prince at Rheinsberg, Frederick had been a passionate collector of the masterpieces of Watteau, Pater and Lancret. After ascending the throne in 1740, he continued collecting for the palaces in Berlin and Potsdam. Frederick's predilection for French painters was due both to their artistic qualities and to their subjects, the "fêtes galantes", parties with music and games amidst "natural" park-like surroundings. Alongside paintings, which form both the majority and the artistic focus of his collections, Frederick also collected snuff-boxes and porcelain services, which he would often give as presents as signs of his appreciation or gratitude. Alongside his love

Previous pages: Few people will be immune to the magic of this unique room. The Golden Gallery (room 363) represents one of the culminations of fantastical interior design of Friderician Rococo. A garden ballroom, it was designed by Georg Wenzeslaus von Knobelsdorff (1699–1753), Johann August Nahl the Elder (1710–1781) and Johann Michael Hoppenhaupt (1709–post 1750). The gallery, 42 metres long and restored between 1961 and 1973, is structured by the gilt decor in the form of shells, tendrils, flowers and fruits, which, in harmony with the figurative depictions of the elements and seasons, create a net-like pattern covering the green marble-effect stucco of the walls, turning this splendid ballroom into a green-and-gold dream garden.

Dance, music, an imaginary park landscape, the very epitome of Rococo serenity … Antonie Pesne (1683–1757) painted this full-length portrait of the famous Italian dancer Barbara Campanini, known as Barbarina, in about 1745. Frederick II was much taken by her talent and grace, and invited her to join the ensemble at his opera house in the avenue known as Unter den Linden, where she soon began to enthral the court as well. This well-known painting formerly hung in the King's Study in the Berlin City Palace.

In just eight days in 1720, "to loosen up his fingers", Antoine Watteau (1684–1721) completed his last masterpiece, the shop signboard for the art dealer Gersaint. It was acquired by Frederick II in 1745, and is still in his Concert Room, where he originally had it hung. The painting did indeed serve as a signboard on the Pont Notre-Dame in Paris before its format was changed and it was cut in half and put back together again. In outstanding painterly fashion, it gives an ironically mocking view of the Paris art scene in the years following the death of Louis XIV.

The "Embarkment for Cythera" by Antoine Watteau (1684–1721), masterpiece painted in 1718/19, was acquired by Frederick the Great for the Potsdam City Palace between 1752 and 1765. The motif could be said to anticipate the coming social upheavals by pointing to the power of love to break down class barriers. A diverse party of pilgrims has enjoyed the amorous and sensuous pleasures of the island of Cythera, synonymous in the 18th century with an earthly paradise, and is now about to board the golden barque for the journey home.

for works of art in porcelain and precious stones, it was not least economic considerations that moved the king in 1763 to acquire for the Prussian state the porcelain factory of Johann Ernst Gotzkowsky, later – and to this day – known as the Königliche Porzellanmanufaktur Berlin or KPM: the Royal Porcelain Factory in Berlin.

Tabatières, elaborate snuff-boxes decorated with precious stones, were among Frederick II's favourite objects. He owned more than 300. The king's youngest sister Amalie reports that he often gave her a "pinch" out of one of his numerous boxes, and that he always had one on him. Anyone receiving such a jewel as a gift could be sure he stood high in the king's favour. The Charlottenburg golden snuff-box with its portrait of the young Frederick framed in diamond roses was presented by the king to Prince Leopold of Anhalt-Dessau in recognition of his military services (room 356).

Frederick the Great commissioned impressive porcelain services, some of which are now kept in the Court Table and Silver Chamber (room 224) at Charlottenburg. The "overturned flower-basket" on a service made for Charlottenburg Palace by KPM in 1770/72 is a common motif of the Friderician Rococo. The choice of motif for the Berlin porcelain service with mythological stories for Charlottenburg Palace, produced in iron-red and gold in 1783, draws on Ovid's poems. They conspicuously correspond with the decorations on the door-panels of the White Hall, which was used as a dining hall (room 362).

At the same time as the king's First Apartment, 1740/42, an apartment for his consort Elizabeth Christine was completed in the New Wing on the basis of Knobelsdorff's plans. The queen probably seldom used the rooms, because although they lived together in Rheinsberg when he was crown prince, they lived apart once he became king. When he ascended the throne in 1740, he made Elizabeth Christine a gift of Schönhausen Palace to the north of Berlin's city centre. She was to use it as her regular summer residence until her death in 1797.

Elizabeth Christine's Charlottenburg suite originally comprised seven rooms, decorated with a modest degree of giltwork and illusionist painting.

Today, all that remains as a witness to the queen's modest apartments is the Japanese Chamber. Following the destruction wrought by the war, the original, bizarrely painted panelling of this room was discovered behind burnt wall-hangings and carefully restored.

The queen spent the long winter months at the Berlin City Palace. Her apartment on the third floor housed numerous paintings, including a series of excellent portraits of ladies of the Prussian court. Painted by Antoine Pesne, they can now be admired in the Blue Anteroom at Charlottenburg, in Frederick the Great's First Apartment. In the brilliant painterly reproduction of the shimmering silks and costly jewellery, Pesne was paying homage to the flattering ideal of beauty prevalent in Friderician Rococo.

Elizabeth Christine, daughter of Duke Ferdinand Albrecht II of Brunswick-Bevern, married Crown Prince Frederick in 1733 at the behest of the "Soldier King" Frederick William I. This unhappy marriage, in which she increasingly had to put up with humiliating neglect, was childless. In this first official portrait of the queen, painted c.1740 by Antoine Pesne (1683–1757) she is depicted in a uniform-like dress with silver embroidery. As a sign of marital fidelity, she holds two carnations to her bosom. The portrait can be seen in Rheinsberg Palace, where she led a carefree life at Frederick's side before he ascended the throne.

In 1691 Frederick III, as Elector of Brandenburg, acquired Schönhausen Palace, today known as Niederschönhausen, from the Dohna family. When Frederick the Great presented it to his consort in 1740, he wrote to her: "You shall be satisfied with me next year, Madame, I shall do everything in my power to help you decorate it entirely to your taste." This 1787 gouache by Carl Benjamin Schwarz (1757–1813) shows the palace, re-designed by Johann Boumann the Elder (1706–1776), from the garden side.

The wall-paintings in the Japanese Chamber (room 313) illustrate a Far Eastern fantasy world of rocaille and vege-- motifs in which exotic figures live fairy-tale lives. They are the work of the painter and engraver Friedrich Wilhelm Höder (d. 1761), who specialized in the chinoiserie genre an idealized image of the Orient. The richly carved and gilded table was designed by Johann August Nahl the Eld (1710–1781) in about 1745.

Three of the eight ladies whom Antoine Pesne (1683–1757) painted for Queen Elizabeth Christine's Gallery of Beauties between 1741 and 1746. On the right is Sophia Maria, Countess of Voss, in hunting gear. She became a maid-of-honour to Queen Sophia Dorothea, the consort o Frederick William I, at the age of 15, and at a great age she was still Chief Lady-in-Waiting to Queen Louisa. Her memoirs, "69 Years at the Prussian Court", constitute a revealing document of the age. The lady in the middle, playing a theorbo, is Eleonore, Baroness von Keyserlingk, who was matron-of-honour to Queen Elizabeth Christine Like her husband Dietrich von Keyserlingk, she was one o Frederick the Great's circle of friends at Rheinsberg when he was crown prince. The lady in the black dress is holdin a mask in her right hand, symbolizing the fancy-dress bal so popular at court. The portraits hang in the Blue Ante-room in the New Wing (room 229).

Charlottenburg Palace in the Late 18th Century

Exotic worlds and early Prussian Neoclassicism— the apartments of King Frederick William II in the New Wing

Frederick William II, the nephew and successor of Frederick the Great, had developed a predilection for Charlottenburg while he was still heir to the throne. In 1788, he had a summer apartment fitted out on the ground floor of the New Wing.

In 1789 Anton Graff (1736–1813), a painter born in Switzerland, executed this portrait of Frederick William II. The artist depicts not some idealized ruler but a human being, literally "warts and all". Frederick William II, who reigned during the transition between Rococo and Neoclassicism, was a patron and lover of the arts, but has gone down in popular memory as a vacillating monarch, much given to the pleasures of the flesh. Political decisions resulting in the loss of much of Prussia's military power, two marriages, numerous mistresses, including his lifelong favourite "beautiful Wilhelmine" Encke, and not least his tendency to mysticism, have all contributed to this image.

Wilhelmine Encke's seductive sensuousness is apparent from this 1776 portrait by Anna Dorothea Therbusch (1721–1782), on display at the Marble Palace in Potsdam. The sitter was the daughter of a waldhorn player from Dessau and met the future Frederick William II in 1766 when she was 13. As his lover and lifelong confidante, she came to exert considerable influence over him. Even after the intimate association began to cool in the 1780s after the birth of several children, she and the king remained friends until his death in 1797. In 1782, Wilhelmine entered into a fictitious marriage with the chamberlain Friedrich Ritz, and in 1792 was ennobled as Countess von Lichtenau.

In order to carry out his paper-work, Frederick William II could retreat to the "classical" ambience of the Etruscan Room (room 318), whose relaxing atmosphere promoted the intellectual faculties. The Berlin artist Johann Gottfried Niedlich (1766–1837) executed the decorative ceiling painting with its geometric structure, taking his inspiration from motifs found on Greek vases, which also accounts for the terracotta hues. Among the motifs of the English colour-prints in their original gilt frames are scenes from Shakespeare. The mahogany chairs and settees with their horse-hair upholstery were made in Berlin at the end of the 18th century.

The five rooms on the garden side, which formerly belonged to the apartment of Elizabeth Christine, the consort of Frederick the Great, were redesigned in an Etruscan-Oriental style based on classical and exotic exemplars. The king's lifelong favourite, Wilhelmine Encke, the future Countess von Lichtenau, more than likely had a say in the design and furnishing of the Summer Apartment.

Colourful, cheerful and fantastical: that was how the king's summer residence was intended to come across. To our modern eyes, however, the arrangement of decorations and works of art, some of which survived the Second World War, is somewhat unusual. Ceilings and walls painted with Chinese figures, colourful wallpaper and silken wall-hangings, Chinese vases and other porcelain items – all lend the rooms an exotic charm still reminiscent of the Rococo.

By contrast, the Neoclassical elements create a more restful impression. They are in the style of an age which sought its models and inspiration in comprehensive works on Etruscan, Greek and Roman art, and reproduced these models in faithful detail.

Right: Those who ate in the Dining Room of the Summer Apartment (room 320) could do so beneath the tent-like "roof" of an illusionistic pavilion conjured up by the Italian stage-set designer Bartolomeo Verona (d. 1813) with his wall and ceiling paintings. He achieved this effect in harmony with the fireplaces in the corners and the tall narrow mirrors above them. The Chinese wallpaper, dating from 1820, which replaces the original destroyed in the war, depicts exotic blossoms with numerous birds and well-populated Chinese village scenes. The twelve-branched chandelier dates from the first decade of the 19th century.

In their somewhat eccentric and reticent elegance, the rooms of the Winter Apartment form an ensemble altogether in tune with the age of early Prussian Neoclassicism.

The existing Rococo ceiling paintings were largely retained, but beneath them, the seven original rooms were re-created in 1796/97 in what was then the "modern" taste. The original furniture, tapestries and chandeliers can still be seen in the restored rooms, in spite of the serious damage suffered in the war. The frequent use of wood in the "back to nature" era is characteristic of the rooms, especially the floors, which have particularly sophisticated parquetry designs in native and exotic timbers.

The furnishings and decoration of the Winter Apartment, too, was influenced to a significant degree by Countess Lichtenau, who acquired her artistic taste on a journey to Italy in 1796. Frederick William II did not live to see the completion in 1797 of the exquisite suite of rooms.

The First and Second Hautelice Rooms (rooms 352, 351) are characterized in particular by the tapestries. Frederick II's brother, Prince Henry of Prussia, received them as a present from Louis XVI in 1784, and gave them to his nephew Frederick William II to decorate the Winter Apartment at Charlottenburg. (Haute lisse or lice: a tapestry woven on a handloom with vertically tensed warp threads.) Don Quixote and his adventures form the theme of the originally six-part series, four parts of which are still extant. The large 1795 painting by Friedrich Georg Weitsch (1758–1828) shows Frederick William II's daughters-in-law Louisa and Frederika adorning his bust with a laurel wreath, honouring him as the begetter of the Peace of Basle. The commode with its inlay work and bronze ornamentation was made c.1785 by Johann Gottlob Fiedler (1735–post 1797).

Without doubt Prussia's most famous sisters, Frederika and Queen Louisa, are depicted in the small version of the well-known life-size marble of the princesses by Johann Gottfried Schadow (1764–1850). The small biscuit-porcelain group created at the Royal Berlin Porcelain Factory (KPM) in 1796 is still one of the KPM's best-sellers.

In Frederick William II's reconstructed Bedroom (room 350) the curtains of yellow-and-white striped and floral satin conceal the alcove in which the king's bed stood. The suite of stools and settee made of maple carved to look like bamboo, the writing desk with its satinwood top section by David Hacker (1748–1801) and the chandelier with its frosted-glass shade, from the Berlin workshop of Werner and Mieth, are among the original furniture and fittings. Numerous small pastel portraits depict members of the Hohenzollern family.

Frederick William II wanted good views from his Charlottenburg garden realm, so in 1788 he had this Belvedere built as an elaborate three-storey observation tower on an oval ground plan, with high-quality interior decor and furniture. Above the ground-floor bedroom with its apple-green satin wall-hangings, there was a sumptuous room panelled with yew and other fine timbers. In the seclusion of this building, which was originally located on an island, the king, who believed in spirit manifestations, was said to take part in Rosicrucian séances. After the war, only the outer walls of the Belvedere were left standing; in the process of reconstruction, the interior was greatly simplified, and since 1971 has served as the Museum of the History of Berlin Porcelain.

The Belvedere and the Theatre

Two striking buildings in the grounds of Charlottenburg Palace, the Theatre at the western end of the Great Orangery and the Belvedere in the northern part of the Palace Garden, still remind us of the age of Frederick William II, his enthusiasm for drama, and his predilection for the English landscape garden and its numerous "follies". These two buildings were erected in the late 18th century following plans drawn up by Carl Gotthard Langhans, the architect who pioneered early Neoclassicism in Prussia and designed Berlin's hallmark, the Brandenburg Gate.

In complete contrast to his uncle, who preferred French art and literature, the king loved and promoted German-language theatre and opera. The exterior of the Charlottenburg Theatre Building, which was almost totally destroyed in the Second World War, unites Baroque and Neoclassical stylistic elements. In the summer of 1797, a few months before his death, Frederick William II, by then seriously ill, attended a performance here for the last time. In the presence of the Turkish ambassador, he watched the German comedy "Sidonia the Magician". The Rev. Johann Christian Gottfried Dressel noted in his Charlottenburg Chronicle that the sight of the king, who was suffering from dropsy, aroused great pity. As long ago as 1902, the interior of the Theatre was put to a different use as a furniture storeroom. Today the building, fully restored externally, is a Museum of Prehistory and Early History.

Charlottenburg Palace in the 19th Century

The royal family idyll – Frederick William III and Louisa at Charlottenburg

By the time Frederick William III, who was married to Louisa of Mecklenburg-Strelitz, ascended the throne in 1797, the Enlightenment and the French Revolution had transformed notions of monarchical display. The lifestyle of the young royal couple was oriented towards bourgeois values. Their apartments at Charlottenburg, especially those of the king, were furnished simply. Queen Louisa used the recently completed Winter Apartment of her late father-in-law on the upper storey of the New Wing, while her husband moved into the apartments of Queen Elizabeth Christine on the ground floor. The by now old-fashioned Rococo decorations disappeared behind wallpaper and coats of paint. As for the furniture, they largely used what they had.

The 1799 double portrait of the Prussian royal couple by Friedrich Georg Weitsch (1758–1828) shows Frederick William III and Louisa in the palace gardens at Charlottenburg. Their mutual affection, visible in the tender touching of hands, reflects their heartfelt closeness. When the portrait was exhibited at the Berlin Academy in 1800, the poet Novalis saw in the royal couple personal role-models for public and family life in Prussia.

The Bedroom of Queen Louisa (room 347) at Charlottenburg was refurnished in 1810 to a design by Karl Friedrich Schinkel (1781–1841). In accordance with Romantic sensibility, the walls are hung with delicate white voile in front of pink wallpaper, hinting at "nature" in the sense of morning mist and rosy-fingered dawn. The elegant bed and the two occasional tables are of pear-wood.

The sweetness and grace of the 26-year-old Louisa are reflected in this well-known 1802 portrait by Josef Grassi (1758–1838). The legendary veneration accorded her was due not just to her beauty, but also to her commitment to Prussia's rescue from Napoleon at Tilsit in 1807. That Charlottenburg was one of her favourite places, we learn from a letter to Tsar Alexander I dated 21 May 1806: "I very much wish you could be here, my dear cousin, and could enjoy the magic of enchanting Charlottenburg, and judge it for yourself. My beloved balcony, which you unfortunately saw covered in snow and ice, is divine again, and I hereby invite you once more to take breakfast with me here. The tea will be excellent, and the eggs quite fresh. If that were possible, how happy I would be!"

The antechamber (Room 317) of Frederick William III's apartments is furnished with important French works of art dominated by the magnificent equestrian portrait "Consul Napoleon Bonaparte Crossing the St. Bernhard Pass", painted in 1800 by Jacques Louis David (1748–1825). It was presented to the King by Field Marshal Gebhard Leberecht von Blücher following the Wars of Liberation. The painting "The Dedication of the Prussian Flag in the Presence of the Allied Sovereigns and Generals on the Champ de Mars in Paris in 1814" by Carle Vernet (1758–1835 or 1836) was commissioned by King Frederick William III to commemorate an event which took place during the allied occupation of Paris following their victory over Napoleon. Karl Friedrich Schinkel (1781–1841) designed the black polished chairs with the golden eagle relief on the back. The magnificent Medici crater vases manufactured in Sèvres were official gifts presented by Charles X of France to the King of Prussia. The round mahogany occasional table with a dark marble top was purchased by Frederick William III in Paris.

The family life of the royals – they were blessed with seven growing children over the years – was exemplary. Major changes ensued only with the outbreak of the Napoleonic Wars. After Prussia's crushing defeats at Jena and Auerstedt in 1806, Frederick William III fled with his family to Memel in East Prussia (now Klaipeda in Lithuania). Napoleon was able to march into Berlin without a fight and set up his quarters for a while at Charlottenburg. A major change in the decoration and furnishing of individual rooms was only undertaken in 1810, when the royal family returned from exile. In this connexion, the young architect Karl Friedrich Schinkel was commissioned to design a bedroom for Queen Louisa.

The Mausoleum and the New Pavilion

The popular queen died on 19 July 1810 at the age of just 34. The grieving widower had a mausoleum built for her in one of her favourite places in the Palace Gardens, at the end of an avenue of silver firs (since replaced by Douglas firs). The little building, based on a Doric temple, was the brainchild of the king; it was built by Heinrich Gentz under Schinkel's supervision. Between 1811 and 1814, Christian Daniel Rauch created the important funerary monument to Louisa in the Hall of Remembrance. The Mausoleum later

UND VERDAMMT DIE SEELE ERRETTEN. Hebr. 10 v 39

DAS GEDAECHTNIS DER GERECHTEN BLEIBT IM SEGEN. Spr 10 v 7

SEELIG IST D...
WIRD ER DIE KRONE

The Mausoleum in the Charlottenburg Palace Gardens was built in 1810 and originally had a temple-like sandstone façade. Replaced by granite in 1828, it found a new purpose as a Hall of Remembrance for Queen Louisa on Peacock Island.

received the mortal remains of Frederick William III (in 1840), and of the first German imperial couple, William I and Augusta.

After Louisa's death, the king avoided the rooms in the New Wing. Following his re-marriage (to Augusta of Harrach) he commissioned Schinkel with the construction of a private summer retreat on the banks of the River

Left: The funerary monument to Queen Louisa, sculpted from Carrara marble by Christian Daniel Rauch (1777–1857), is one of the most moving works of Neoclassical sculptural art in Berlin. It depicts the late queen on a sarcophagus not as dead, but sleeping: idealized, natural, and sovereign.

Right: In the Hall of Remembrance of the Mausoleum is a plaster cast of a marble bust by Christian Daniel Rauch (1777–1857). Carved in 1816 at the behest of Frederick William III, it was to depict the late queen, who had died six years earlier, as she was in life. This was also in accord with the wishes of the growing number of those who venerated her. For his portrait, Rauch adopted the coiffure, the palmette diadem and the classical apparel from his funerary monument. The added veil however reinforces the melancholy expression of dignity, mildness and gentle grief apparent in the slight inclination of the head, the dreamy gaze, and the serious mouth. The bust did not fail to make its effect on the beholder. It was widely disseminated in marble copies, iron and bronze casts, and was set up as a patriotic symbol in both interiors and atmospheric garden nooks, such as on Louisa Island at Charlottenburg.

Top left: Frederick William III's New Pavilion was built under the supervision of Albrecht Dietrich Schadow to plans by Karl Friedrich Schinkel (1781–1841). The model for the cubic building on the banks of the Spree was a villa in Naples which the king had occupied in 1822. The building was destroyed in the war but later reconstructed, and since 1970 has housed a collection of high-quality art dating from Schinkel's time, including major Romantic and Biedermeier paintings, including works by Caspar David Friedrich (1774–1840), Karl Friedrich Schinkel (1781–1841), Carl Blechen (1798–1840) and Eduard Gaertner (1801–1877), together with early 19th-century sculpture, furniture, and crafts.

In the Garden Hall of the New Pavilion (room 12/13) the semicircular bench is reminiscent of classical models, and, in conjunction with the marble-effect stucco walls, the fireplaces and the Carrara-marble busts, creates a Mediterranean effect.

Far left: After he had been a widower for 14 years, Frederick William III contracted a morganatic marriage in Charlottenburg Palace Chapel in 1824 with the 24-year-old Austrian countess Augusta of Harrach, who became Princess von Liegnitz and Countess von Hohenzollern.
At first suspiciously rejected by the rest of the royal family, the reticent and modest young woman soon won the affection of all. This portrait of the Princess shows her riding in the gardens of Charlottenburg Palace. It was painted as a birthday present for her husband in c.1838 by Franz Krüger (1797–1857).

Left: In a "uniform portrait" painted c.1835 by Franz Krüger (1797–1857), Frederick William III, who came across as sober and often inhibited, appears in monumentally heroic attitude against the background of a dramatically clouded horizon with Charlottenburg Palace visible on the left.

This "Interior View of the Palm House on Peacock Island", commissioned by Frederick William III, was painted between 1832 and 1834 by Carl Blechen (1798–1840). The building itself was unfortunately destroyed by fire in 1880. It was erected at the behest of the king in 1830/31 to accommodate his newly acquired plant collection. The female figures dressed in oriental attire reclining beneath the palm fronds convey a tropical fairy-tale atmosphere, which satisfied the curiosity of the Prussian court about exotic cultures and foreign lands at the beginning of the 19th century. The painting is displayed along with other important works by Blechen in the King's former library (Room 311) in his apartment on the ground floor of the New Wing.

Spree in 1824/25. This New Pavilion, as it was called, an almost cubic two-storey building with a flat roof, French windows and all-round balcony, was based on Italian models. The interior decoration and furniture are regarded as the archetype of elegant Prussian Neoclassicism in the manner of Schinkel.

The life of a grand seigneur in the country –
Frederick William IV and Queen Elizabeth
at Charlottenburg

From 1841/42, the Baroque central section of Charlottenburg Palace was used once more by Frederick William III's successor, Frederick William IV, and his consort, Elizabeth of Bavaria. They occupied two apartments on the

upper floor of the Old Palace in which the "soldier king", Frederick William I, had lived as crown prince, and which Frederick the Great had used as temporary accommodation until the New Wing was finished.

    Frederick William IV moved into six rooms to the west of the Upper Oval Hall, while the queen chose the suite of rooms to the east. The king had been familiar with these quarters from his youth, using them during his parents' frequent periods of residence at Charlottenburg. He now commissioned the architect Johann Heinrich Strack to redesign them in part, using furniture from various epochs. "The style of the royal household at Charlottenburg was that of a grand seigneur in his country house," wrote Otto von Bismarck in 1852 in his "Thoughts and Memoirs", and went on to say that he had been compensated for a delayed audience here by "a good and elegantly served breakfast".

    At first the royal couple resided at Charlottenburg only during the autumn and winter months, but following the 1848 revolution, they spent more and more time here, as the town was more loyal than Berlin. After Frederick William IV's death in 1861, his widow Elizabeth continued to use the Palace until her own death in 1873.

The Berlin painter Karl Wilhelm Wach (1787–1845) portrayed Frederick William IV, the "romantic on the Prussian throne", and his ardently loving queen Elizabeth in 1840, when he succeeded his father. Though full of lofty ideals, with a very broad education, and artistically talented, the king was however mentally equipped to deal neither with the political problems of the age nor with the social questions raised by the ongoing industrial revolution. Apathetic and, after several strokes, seriously ill, he was forced to hand over the business of government to his younger brother, later William I, in 1858.

Right: Frederick William IV's Charlottenburg Library (room 203) was fitted out in 1845/46 with maple-veneer panelling and matching furniture to a design by Johann Heinrich Strack (1805–1880). The cosy atmosphere of the room is largely determined by the stove with its white glazed tiles, produced by the pottery works of Tobias Christoph Feilner (1773–1839). Damaged in the Second World War, the room was restored with the original furniture, which had been saved.

In Frederick William IV's Adjutant Room (room 206), landscape paintings of South American rain forests by Ferdinand Bellermann (1814–1889) recall the momentous travels of the naturalist Alexander von Humboldt, who belonged to the king's inner circle of friends. The gilt chairs and the elegant mahogany table were designed by Karl Friedrich Schinkel (1781–1841) for the royal couple's apartments in the Berlin City Palace.

"The View of a Harbour" painted by Caspar David Friedrich (1774–1840) c.1815 was a birthday present for the 21-year-old crown prince from his father Frederick William III. By 1840, the masterpiece of Romantic painting was hanging in Frederick William IV's Charlottenburg apartment. As paintings by Caspar David Friedrich usually have a deeper symbolic meaning, the ships at anchor or putting into the harbour at dusk may well signify the end of man's journey through life. Today the painting is on display alongside further masterpieces by C.D. Friedrich in Frederick William III's New Pavilion.

Paintings with Italian views, Biedermeier genre scenes and still-lifes, a gilt tapestry-covered suite from the Berlin City Palace and a Boulle cabinet with a KPM floral-pattern porcelain service in Queen Elizabeth's Green Room (room 212) are typical of princely living in the mid-19th century. Almost totally destroyed during the Second World War, the apartments of Frederick William IV and his consort could only be restored in simplified form, using works of art taken from the royal couple's other palaces.

In 1847 Gottfried Wilhelm Voelcker (1775–1849), a famous painter of flowers at the KPM, composed an intoxicating Biedermeier garden dream for Queen Elizabeth's apartment at Charlottenburg (room 212).

Imperial Charlottenburg from 1871 to 1918

Neither William I, the brother of Frederick William IV and his successor as King of Prussia, and from 1871 the first German Emperor, nor his consort Augusta showed much interest in Charlottenburg, apart from the Mausoleum, which he frequently visited. It had become a national shrine, being the last resting place of his mother Queen Louisa, who had achieved almost saintly status among the people. The last ruler from the House of Hohenzollern to actually live at Charlottenburg, albeit briefly, was his son Emperor Frederick III, who reigned for a few months in 1888 with his consort Victoria, the eldest daughter of Queen Victoria of England. After that Charlottenburg was only used occasionally for receptions and to accommodate aristocratic guests at major family celebrations.

On 19 July 1870, the 60th anniversary of the death of his mother Queen Louisa, having received the French declaration of war, King William I of Prussia visited the Charlottenburg Mausoleum. In his 1873 sketch for a painting, Anton von Werner (1843–1915) depicted the king deep in contemplation next to the sarcophagus of the queen, praying for strength in the impending campaign.

On this photograph taken in 1888, the imperial standard on the Palace Tower signals the presence of Emperor Frederick III in his Charlottenburg residence.

In the spring of 1888, the already seriously ill Emperor Frederick III, together with his consort Victoria, moved into the former apartments of King Frederick William IV and Queen Elizabeth on the top floor of Charlottenburg Palace. The liberal monarch, who was destined to reign for just 99 days, did not live to introduce a parliamentary system on the English model into Germany. The Empress Frederick, as Victoria was known after the death of her beloved husband, like her mother-in-law Empress Augusta, in her vigorous rejection of Prussia's military and power-political tradition, was vehemently opposed to the imperial chancellor, Otto von Bismarck. Heinrich von Angeli (1840–1925) portrayed the couple in 1874, while Frederick was still crown prince. Victoria's Renaissance-style garments can be understood as an allusion to her patronage of the arts.

The brief reign of Frederick III witnessed a major event at Charlottenburg. In April 1888, the Empress's mother, Queen Victoria of England, paid a visit. A woodcut by R. Tailor (fl. 1870–1900) depicts her arrival at the palace. She was accommodated in Frederick the Great's Second Apartment in the New Wing.

The Court Silver Chamber

Like all European courts, the Prussian ruling house maintained at its most important palaces Silver Chambers, in which costly cutlery, candlesticks, vases and table decorations were kept. Silverware, porcelain services and gilt bronze articles for the court table were mostly kept in rooms close to the kitchen. The stock of silver was much diminished by the melting-down of items in times of war and distress. When in 1926 the contents of the Silver Chamber were handed over to ex-Emperor William II, who was living in exile in Doorn in Holland, the Prussian palaces finally lost their last remaining silver. The Silver Chamber at Charlottenburg today contains items on loan from the Doorn Foundation together with significant new items acquired in recent years. Selected examples provide an overview of the history of table decoration from the Baroque, via the Friderician silver and porcelain services, to the pomp of the 19th century. The last set of court silver to be made, between 1904 and 1914, was the "Crown Prince Silver", which comprises 50 place-settings.

In June 1904, the engagement was announced of the Prussian crown prince William, the eldest son of Emperor William II, to Cecilia, Duchess zu Mecklenburg. The coloured photograph was taken in the Berlin studio of Emil Bieber (1878–1963). Cecilienhof Palace in Potsdam, built between 1913 and 1917 and named after the Crown Princess, was occupied by the couple until 1945.

The "Crown Prince Silver" was commissioned by 414 Prussian towns and cities as a wedding present for William and Cecilia. It comprised more than 600 pieces and was designed for a table 16 metres in length. The completion of the silver in 1914 coincided with the outbreak of the First World War. After the abdication of the Hohenzollern dynasty, it never came into the possession of the princely couple. In 1928, it was acquired by Berlin City Council on condition that it be put on public display. It is now exhibited as a loan from the Berlin State government (room 235). The middle of the table is covered along its entire length by a mirror, on which stand flower bowls, figural table decorations and candelabra. Between the place settings there stand, alternately, carafes with silver coasters and bowls for sweetmeats. Numerous artists and craftspeople were involved in the design and execution of the silver. The figural decorations were largely the work of Ignatius Taschner (1871–1913), the cutlery of Emil Lettré (1876–1954). Stylistically the "Crown Prince Silver" shows the influence both of Art Nouveau and of Neoclassicism.

Charlottenburg Palace in the 20th Century

The end of Hohenzollern rule

The palaces under state management

War damage and post-war reconstruction

Charlottenburg shared the same fate as many other palaces which, after the end of the monarchy in 1918, were put for a time to different use: in its case, it became a field hospital. Following an initiative supported by prominent personalities to preserve outstanding Hohenzollern palaces, Charlottenburg, together with its gardens and park buildings, was placed in the care of the State Palace and Garden Administration in 1927, with a view to its becoming a museum. A few years later, its propaganda potential was exploited by the Nazis, especially during the 1936 Olympic Games. In 1943, large parts of the palace were destroyed or seriously damaged by Royal Air Force bombing raids. However, much of the contents had already been moved for safe keeping elsewhere, and in 1946, the first steps were taken towards protecting some of the rooms against the ravages of winter, and thus towards an eventual reconstruction. Restoration work on the interior started in the 1950s and continued in a number of phases into the 1990s, in part in contemporary style. An ongoing problem is the reacquisition of the original works of art, which, happily, has been accelerated by the re-unification of Germany and the establishment in 1995 of the Stiftung Preußische Schlösser und Gärten Berlin-Brandenburg.

During the 1936 Berlin Olympic Games, the Hitler regime sought to cast itself in a positive light to the visitors from all over the world. State receptions also took place at Charlottenburg, in particular in the Golden Gallery. In 1937, Reich Marshal Hermann Göring organized an open-air evening performance by the ballet company of the State Opera House on the lawn in front of the garden façade. The illumination was provided by Luftwaffe searchlights.

On the evening of 22 November 1943, Berlin suffered its heaviest air-raid, as a result of which Charlottenburg Palace was also severely damaged. The Old Palace was hit, the top storey of the central section being completely, and the ground floor largely destroyed. The domed tower collapsed, while the wings to the east and west of the central section also suffered serious damage. Among the eye-witnesses were the two sons of Palace Inspector Bahr, who spent the night in the air-raid shelter beneath the tower. They reported that their father had rescued works of art from the burning palace before the ceiling collapsed. A photograph taken four days later shows the extent of the destruction.

The reconstruction of Charlottenburg Palace would have been inconceivable without the commitment and energy of the first post-war administrator Margarete Kühn and her staff. Thanks to her seeing eye-to-eye on technical matters with the art-protection officer of the British occupying forces, the palace ruins were soon classified as a so-called "command building", which meant that funds were made available for urgent restoration measures.

An outstanding example of how the restorers of the palace interior did not shy away from new solutions, some of them controversial: the ceiling painting of the White Hall (room 362) in the New Wing executed in 1972/73 by Hann Trier (1915–1999). It replaces the Rococo ceiling painting lost in the war by a contemporary abstract composition recalling the delicate style of Antoine Pesne (1683–1757).

Charlottenburg Palace Gardens

Baroque garden design, an "English" landscape garden, post-war restoration

In front of the palace façade the reconstructed French-style formal garden opens out in majestic fashion. In the absolutist ideology of the Baroque period, even nature was subordinate to the will of the rulers, its artistic shaping being understood as an open-air continuation of the palace interior.

Following page, top: On this etching by Martin Engelbrecht (1684–1756) based on the ideal design (c.1717) by Johann Friedrich Eosander (1669–1728), we have a bird's-eye view of Charlottenburg. However, the two wings on the near side of the courtyard railings were never actually built, nor did the gardens reach quite this extent.

The early stages of the 55-hectare Charlottenburg Palace Gardens are closely tied up with the building of the little Lietzenburg summer residence. Even while she was still Electress of Brandenburg, the future Queen Sophia Charlotte of Prussia had indicated her particular interest in garden design. Starting in 1697 she had an elaborate park laid out on the model of Versailles by Siméon Godeau: it was one of Germany's first French-style Baroque gardens. The Orangery was particularly famous, with its more than 500 orange and lemon trees, whose intoxicating scent during the summer months filled the formal area in front of the Great Orangery. Godeau, a pupil of André Le Nôtre, structured the extensive grounds into three hierarchically graded areas. The approx. 500-metre terrace along the garden front of the palace was adorned by statues, vases and potted plants. Perpendicular to this, the main axis close to the palace

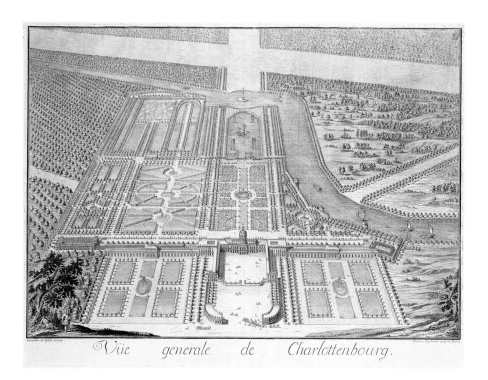

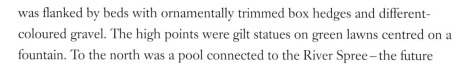

Vüe generale de Charlottenbourg.

was flanked by beds with ornamentally trimmed box hedges and different-coloured gravel. The high points were gilt statues on green lawns centred on a fountain. To the north was a pool connected to the River Spree – the future

Below: A view across the Orangery Garden, with the statues of the goddesses Flora and Pomona, towards the Orangery and the dome.

Left-hand page, top right: The miniature-like painting after a portrait by Gedéon Romandon (d. 1697) depicts Sophia Charlotte in about 1691, when she was still electress, against an architectural background with floral decorations and dolphin fountains. Charlottenburg owes its Baroque garden complex, designed by Siméon Godeau (1632–post 1716), to her passion for horticulture.

Right: During the summer months, when the potted plants were put outside in the Baroque garden, the Great Orangery provided a splendid venue for court festivities. An etching after Johann Friedrich Eosander (1669–1728) shows the high vaulted ceiling decorated with allegories of the seasons, the signs of the zodiac, and the four elements, in the Central Salon with its columns. After its destruction in the war and subsequent reconstruction, the Great Orangery today is a favourite spacious venue for state receptions, cultural events and private functions.

"The Orangery and table were illuminated with 1,200 wax candles and embellished on both sides with orange and other trees." This was the description by a contemporary observer of the decoration of the Great Orangery on the occasion of the marriage of Princess Frederika Louisa, a sister of Frederick the Great. Antonie Pesne (1683–1757) has here portrayed her with her groom, Frederick, Margrave of Brandenburg-Ansbach.

Bizarre botanical treasures such as the "Deformed Red Tulip", painted in c.1705 by Willem Frederik van Royen (1645–1723) and today one of the older paintings to be found at Charlottenburg, doubtless adorned the Baroque garden.

On the edge of the earthenware pot with three lilies—the work of an unknown master—is written "Die Blum. Aron. oder Bfaffen. Pint. in Scharlotten Burg Anno 1735".

Carp Pond. This was also a harbour for gondolas. To the west of the beds were further geometric beds bordered by trimmed hornbeam hedges.

No French Baroque garden could be without its canal, and so there was one here too. Particularly important, though, was the visual-axis system, which led the eye beyond the garden area as such into the countryside beyond, designed to symbolize that the power of Frederick I as an absolute monarch also extended over the natural world. The Prussian rulers, even the parsimonious "soldier king" Frederick William I, used the Orangery and the gardens for major court festivities and magnificent weddings. The Spree provided an ideal means of access by water, enabling the royal family and their guests

to proceed in gilt barges from the Berlin City Palace to Charlottenburg, and to wander around the splendid Baroque gardens there to the sound of music, dancing and fireworks. Right up until the death of Frederick the Great, the gardens were regularly maintained, and in part modernized, but not fundamentally altered.

It was only under Frederick William II and Frederick William III that gradually the formal French garden was transformed into a landscape garden on the English model. By 1833, virtually nothing remained of the Baroque layout. The new grassy meadows were broken up by picturesque copses, meandering paths, isolated statues in flower-beds, and dreamy watercourses around islands which could only be reached by rope-ferries on the model of the garden complex at Wörlitz. The Baroque system of avenues was however never completely swept away. The changes in the gardens were carried out according to plans drawn up by Johann August Eyserbeck, Georg Steiner, and Peter Joseph Lenné. At the end of the 18th century, Frederick William II, entirely in the spirit of the age of "sensibility", had two further buildings erected, neither of which has been preserved: the Gothic Anglers' Lodge on the Spree, and the Tahitian Wickerwork House as a place of retreat for a courtly society that dreamed of a "natural" life in ideal South Sea surroundings.

In the mid-19th century, the spirit of Revivalism during the reign of Frederick William IV led to a certain degree of ornamental restoration in

Laid out in well-considered symmetry, the tender citrus plants still overwinter every year in the Small Orangery, their traditional place.

On this gouache by an unknown artist, painted sometime after 1786, we see, in addition to the majestic garden façade with its rich array of sculptures on the terrace, workers performing the laborious task of shifting the plants in their pots.

When the gardens were re-designed in what was then the modern landscape style, the straight banks of the Carp Pond were relaxed and given a setting of copses and shrubberies.

the Neo-Baroque style. After the death of Frederick III, the palace lost its importance for the Hohenzollern, a loss reflected in the state of the gardens.

At the end of the Second World War, not only were the palace and the outbuildings in ruins, but the gardens too were totally devastated. The former ornamental garden was for a time used for growing crops, but between

This etching by Friedrich Wilhelm Meyer (b. c.1770), dating from 1805/06 and based on a drawing by Heinrich Anton Dähling (1773–1850), depicts Frederick William III with his family in the Charlottenburg Palace Gardens. At the centre of this idyllic conversation-piece in the midst of "nature" sits the king. It is his birthday (3 August), and he is to be presented with garlands of flowers by the crown prince (the future Frederick William IV) and his sisters. Queen Louisa and her sister-in-law Marianne are coifed and dressed in the latest fashion, inspired by Classical Greece. The venue of this family party could be the New Island, created in 1799 as a "romantic isle", which was renamed after Queen Louisa following her death in 1810, when a bronze bust to a design by Christian Daniel Rauch (1770–1857) was set up there in memory of the unforgettable queen.

In 1846 Eduard Gaertner (1801–1877) succeeded in masterly fashion in capturing the carefree atmosphere of a summer stroll on the terrace of Charlottenburg Palace during the time of Frederick William IV.

1952 and 1968 restored to its Baroque formality framed by avenues of lime trees, with an octagonal pool and fountain at the main axis crossing.

After more than 30 years of use, this formal garden is now much more like its historical exemplars. In parts, as with the coloured gravel, modifications have been undertaken, and the ensemble has been completed with cast-iron vases, including four magnificent ones that belonged to Frederick I.

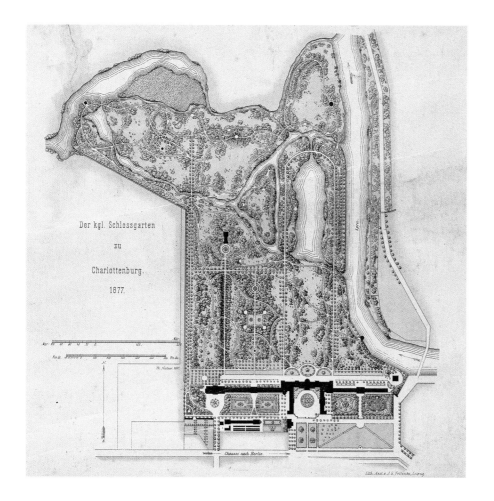

In 1877 Theodor Nietner II (1823–1894) published his "Horticultural Sketchbook" containing a garden plan, which, alongside the landscaping of the late 18th and early 19th centuries, also documents the revival of geometric forms at the time of Frederick William IV.

Spring impressions in the romantic wilderness of the Charlottenburg Palace Gardens, captured in 1908 by Adolf Obst (1869–1945).

Following the restoration of the French-style formal garden in 2001, Berlin once more possesses an example of Baroque garden design unique in the region. The ornamental areas of red, white and black gravel are framed by sumptuous flowerbeds with historical plants, including, in the spring, various tulip varieties, crown imperials, daffodils, English wallflowers, hyacinths and forget-me-nots; and in the summer, roses, lilies and passion-flowers.

Four marble-effect cast-iron vases with the monogram of Frederick I commemorate his coronation in 1701. They flank the main axis, the royal path, in the Baroque formal garden. The majesty of Absolutism is still present in the gardens, too.

With thanks to Erika Luise Preiße for her valuable contribution.

Front cover: Charlottenburg Palace from the courtyard
Front cover flap (outside): Sophia Charlotte, Queen in Prussia, painting by
Friedrich Wilhelm Weidemann, c.1705
Front cover flap (inside): Charlottenburg Palace Garden (cartography © SPSG,
Michael Benecke) and plan of Charlottenburg Palace (plans © Theodor Härtl, Berlin)
Back cover flap (inside): Genealogy of the rulers of the House of Hohenzollern from
Elector Frederick William of Brandenburg to Emperor William II

Photograph acknowledgements: All the illustrations derive from the archive of the Stiftung
Preußische Schlösser und Gärten Berlin-Brandenburg (photographers: Jörg P. Anders; Hans
Bach; Roland Handrick; Andreas Jacobs; Gerhard Klein; Daniel Lindner; Wolfgang Pfauder
and others) with the exception of p.3: Günter Schneider; p.10 top, p.19, p.47 top: © Klaus
Frahm/artur

3rd English edition 2008
© Contents and design: Prestel Verlag, Munich · Berlin · London · New York, 2005

The Library of Congress Cataloguing-in-Publication data is available.

Prestel Verlag, Königinstr. 9, D-80539 München
Tel. +49 (0) 89 24 29 08–300, fax +49 (0) 89 24 29 08–335
info@prestel.de
www.prestel.de
Prestel books are available worldwide. Please contact your nearest bookseller or
write to one of the above addresses for information concerning your local distributor.

Edited by: Jochen Stamm (German text)
Translated from the German by: Michael Scuffil, Leverkusen
Project management: Hansmann+Hausmann, Cologne
Design: Maja Kluy, Munich
Reproductions by: LVD, Berlin
Printed and bound by: GRASPO CZ, a.s.
Printed on chlorine-free bleached paper
Printed in the Czech Republic

ISBN 978-3-7913-3305-2

A view of the gardens of Charlottenburg Palace.